I0017941

From Code To

Consciousness:

The OpenAI

Saga

Unveiling the Story of OpenAI: Bridging
the Gap from Algorithms to True
Consciousness

Jonathan Berkeley

1

All rights reserved. No part of this
publication may be reproduced,
distributed, or transmitted in any form or
by any means, including photocopying,
recording, or other electronic or
mechanical methods, without the prior
written permission of the publisher, except
in the case of brief quotations embodied in
critical reviews and certain other
noncommercial uses permitted by
copyright law.
© Jonathan Berkeley

TABLE OF CONTENTS

OpenAI's Mission in the Field of Artificial Intelligence   **7**

Founding Principles   8

Democratizing Access to Benefits   9

Long-Term Safety   10

Technical Leadership   11

Balancing Long-Term and Short-Term Considerations   12

Chapter 1: Inception   **15**

Founding Members   15

Motivations and Common Ground   20

Early Vision and Formation   21

Collaborative Dynamics   23

Challenges and Lessons Learned   24

Legacy of the Founding Members   25

Chapter 2: Exploring the Genesis of OpenAI and Addressing AI Risks   **27**

The Birth of OpenAI   29

Shaping the Narrative: AGI as a Global Benefit   30

Concerns about AGI Risks   31

OpenAI's Mission as a Response to Concerns   35

Navigating Challenges and Evolving Perspectives   38

Funding Rounds and Financial Backing   41

Legacy of the Early Years   44

Chapter 3: Research Focus - OpenAI's Exploration of Early Projects and Key Technologies   **47**

Foundational Research Areas 48
Early Projects 50
Technical Leadership and Innovation 53
Challenges and Ethical Considerations 55
Collaborative Initiatives 57
Evolution of Key Technologies 58

Chapter 4: Key Milestones - AlphaGo Match: OpenAI's Reaction and Research Impact 61
AlphaGo: A Watershed Moment in AI 62
Impact on OpenAI's Research Agenda 64
Evolving Landscape of AI Development 66
Leveraging Inspiration for Innovation 69

Chapter 5: GPT Series - Evolution of the Generative Pre-trained Transformer 73
GPT-1: Inaugurating a New Era 74
GPT-2: Scaling New Heights 75
GPT-3: Pushing the Boundaries 77
The Evolution of GPT Series: Milestones and Contributions 79
Ethical Considerations and Mitigation Strategies 81
Legacy of the GPT Series 83

Chapter 6: Industry Collaborations - OpenAI's Partnerships and Research Endeavors 87
Key Industry Collaborations 89
Impact on AI Research 92
Challenges and Considerations 94
Collaborative Initiatives and Contributions 96
Evolving Landscape and Future Directions 98
The Philosophy of Open Source at OpenAI 101

Impact on the AI Community   105

Ethical Use and Responsible AI   107

Future Directions and Continuous Innovation
109

**Chapter 7: Controversies, Long-Term Vision,
and Reflections on OpenAI's Journey   113**

Controversies and Criticisms   113

Long-Term Vision and Goals   116

Reflections on OpenAI's Journey   119

Significance in the History of Artificial
Intelligence   122

Conclusion   126

OpenAI's Mission in the Field of Artificial Intelligence

In the rapidly changing field of artificial intelligence, OpenAI is a visible force with a goal that goes beyond innovation and research. Elon Musk, Sam Altman, Greg Brockman, Ilya Sutskever, and others founded OpenAI in December 2015 with a single vision: to ensure that artificial general intelligence (AGI) benefits all of humankind. This review goes into the heart of OpenAI's purpose, delving into its aims, ideals, and the larger ramifications of its AI work.

Founding Principles

The dedication to tackle the substantial impact of artificial general intelligence on society is central to OpenAI's purpose. The founding members were motivated by a realization of the possible hazards connected with AGI as well as a desire to lead its development in a way that prioritizes humanity's well-being. The goal statement of OpenAI, as defined in its Charter, emphasizes that AGI should be utilized for the benefit of all while avoiding enabling applications that might damage humanity or concentrate power excessively.

Democratizing Access to Benefits

One of the core aspects of OpenAI's aim is to ensure that the advantages of AGI are widely dispersed. The deployment of strong AI systems, according to OpenAI, should not result in the concentration of power in the hands of a few. Instead, the nonprofit fights for public access to, control over, and benefits from AI breakthroughs.

OpenAI recognizes the importance of technological leadership in achieving this aim. OpenAI seeks to properly address the impact of AGI on society by being at the forefront of AI capabilities. The group also pledges to aggressively collaborate with other academic and policy institutes, encouraging a collaborative approach to addressing global AGI concerns.

Long-Term Safety

Beyond the creation of sophisticated AI systems, OpenAI's purpose includes a commitment to doing research to make AGI safe. Recognizing the possible hazards and uncertainties connected with the introduction of AGI, OpenAI prioritizes efforts to make AGI safe and to push the adoption of safety research throughout the AI community.

This dedication to safety arises from the realization that as AI systems become more powerful, the significance of safety precautions becomes even more vital. To reduce the hazards of AGI, OpenAI emphasizes the importance of acting attentively and ethically, and the organization is committed to encouraging the adoption of safety research across the AI community.

Technical Leadership

The pursuit of technological leadership in AI capabilities is a crucial component of OpenAI's goal. Without a solid technological base, OpenAI believes that policy and safety advocacy are ineffective. Because OpenAI is at the forefront of AI research and development, it is well positioned to successfully address AGI's impact on society and to accomplish its objective of ensuring that the advantages of AGI are widely dispersed.

OpenAI's approach to cutting-edge research and development reflects the company's dedication to technological leadership. The company is actively involved in a wide range of AI initiatives, from basic research to the creation of commercial applications. OpenAI's multidimensional strategy strives to push the frontiers of AI capabilities while keeping a close eye on safety and ethical factors.

Balancing Long-Term and Short-Term Considerations

The purpose of OpenAI is characterized by a realization of the contradiction between long-term safety and technological growth. The group is dedicated to resolving safety concerns and reducing the dangers related with AGI. However, it also recognizes the necessity for a proactive approach to AI capabilities in order to successfully handle the social consequences of AGI.

This delicate approach entails finding a balance between cutting-edge research and aggressively pushing the widespread adoption of safety precautions. OpenAI understands the need of cooperating with other research and policy institutes to build a global community that solves the issues posed by AGI collectively.

To summarize, OpenAI's aim in the realm of artificial intelligence is broad and forward-thinking. OpenAI's aim extends beyond the limitations of a typical research organization, based on values such as securing the wide advantages of AGI, prioritizing safety research, and retaining technical leadership. OpenAI, as a leading force in the AI community, actively defines the course of AI development, with a vision that embraces cooperation, safety, and humanity's collective well-being in the age of artificial intelligence. The objective of the organization establishes a bold precedent for responsible and ethical AI development, setting the way for a future in which AGI's revolutionary power is harnessed for the benefit of everyone.

Chapter 1: Inception

The launch of OpenAI represented a watershed point in the history of artificial intelligence, technology, and societal influence. OpenAI was created in December 2015 by a collection of significant persons with varied experiences and expertise to lead the development of artificial general intelligence (AGI) for the benefit of humanity. This chapter goes into the histories of the founding members, examining their motivations, experiences, and the distinct set of abilities they contributed to the creation of OpenAI.

Founding Members

Elon Musk

Elon Musk, the visionary entrepreneur and inventor of SpaceX and Tesla, was instrumental in the formation of OpenAI. Musk has been a strong champion for ethical AI research, owing to his ambitious objectives and forward-thinking mentality. His concerns about the possible perils of AGI prompted him to co-found OpenAI as a way to guarantee that the development of artificial intelligence is consistent with ethical and safety concerns.

Musk's engagement in many technology endeavors indicated a strong desire to shape humanity's destiny. His unusual position as a leader in both the space exploration and electric car sectors gave him with a comprehensive view on technology's transformational power and the need for ethical frameworks in its growth.

Altman, Sam

Sam Altman, a well-known entrepreneur and investor, collaborated with Elon Musk to co-found OpenAI. Altman offered tremendous expertise in growing and assisting early-stage firms as the former president of Y Combinator, a notable startup incubator. His enthusiasm for technical advancement, along with a dedication to tackling its societal ramifications, prompted him to become a fundamental architect of OpenAI's goal.

Altman's position in the startup environment, as well as his dedication to promoting innovation, positioned him as a link between the entrepreneurial sector and the developing science of artificial intelligence. His participation demonstrated a dedication to combining technical proficiency with a pragmatic knowledge of how AI affects industry and society.

Brockman, Greg

OpenAI's Chief Technology Officer, Greg Brockman, offered a plethora of technological skills to the founding team. Brockman, who has a background in computer science and software development, was essential in establishing OpenAI's technological vision. His previous expertise as CTO of Stripe, a renowned online payment company, gave a practical layer to OpenAI's purpose.

Brockman's participation highlighted the technical rigor necessary to traverse the intricacies of AGI development. His work with high-profile technology firms gave insights into the obstacles of scaling and implementing cutting-edge technologies, which contributed to OpenAI's comprehensive approach to AI research and development.

Sutskever, Ilya

Ilya Sutskever, a notable researcher in the field of artificial intelligence, joined the founding team with a solid academic background. Sutskever, who holds a Ph.D. in Machine Learning from the University of Toronto, has made substantial contributions to deep learning and neural network research. His knowledge propelled OpenAI to the forefront of AI breakthroughs.

Sutskever's job as OpenAI's Chief Scientist underlined the organization's dedication to rigorous research and innovation. His academic accomplishments, which included co-founding the Google Brain team, established a track record of pushing the frontiers of AI capabilities—an important component in OpenAI's goal of technological leadership.

Motivations and Common Ground

The convergence of these diverse backgrounds and skill sets was driven by a shared concern for the trajectory of AGI development. The founding members recognized the transformative potential of AGI and the need for proactive measures to ensure its responsible deployment. Elon Musk's public statements on the existential risks of unchecked AI development set the tone for OpenAI's mission, framing it as a proactive effort to guide the course of AGI for the benefit of humanity.

The common ground among the founding members was a commitment to combining technical excellence with ethical considerations. While each member brought a unique perspective, the collective goal was to create an organization that could lead in AI capabilities, actively address safety concerns, and collaborate with the broader community to navigate the challenges posed by AGI.

Early Vision and Formation

The early vision of OpenAI was rooted in the belief that AGI should be aligned with human values, transparently developed, and accessible to a broad range of stakeholders. The organization's commitment to using any influence it obtains over AGI's deployment to ensure it benefits all of humanity was enshrined in the OpenAI Charter—a guiding document that outlines the principles and values shaping the organization's mission.

The formation of OpenAI was accompanied by a commitment of financial resources. Elon Musk and other initial donors pledged a substantial amount to fund OpenAI's operations. This financial backing was instrumental in providing the organization with the autonomy and resources needed to pursue its ambitious goals without being beholden to short-term commercial interests.

Collaborative Dynamics

The collaborative dynamics among the founding members played a crucial role in shaping OpenAI's identity. Elon Musk's visionary outlook and commitment to safety were complemented by Sam Altman's pragmatic understanding of entrepreneurship and industry impact. Greg Brockman's technical acumen and experience in leading engineering teams provided the organization with a solid technical foundation, while Ilya Sutskever's expertise in AI research added a rigorous scientific dimension.

The collaborative spirit extended beyond the founding members to include a broader network of advisors, researchers, and contributors. OpenAI's commitment to fostering cooperation with other research and policy institutions reflected a recognition of the collective responsibility to address AGI's challenges.

Challenges and Lessons Learned

The early days of OpenAI were not without challenges. The ambitious nature of the mission, coupled with the inherent uncertainties of AGI development, posed complex hurdles. Balancing the pursuit of technical leadership with long-term safety considerations required navigating a delicate equilibrium. The organization's commitment to transparency and collaboration also raised questions about the practical implementation of its principles.

Lessons learned during this formative period contributed to OpenAI's adaptive approach. Charter updates reflected a commitment to continuous improvement, with the organization actively seeking feedback, iterating on its principles, and refining its strategies based on the evolving landscape of AI research and development.

Legacy of the Founding Members

As OpenAI evolved, the legacy of the founding members remained embedded in its culture and mission. Elon Musk's advocacy for responsible AI development, Sam Altman's pragmatic approach to industry impact, Greg Brockman's technical leadership, and Ilya Sutskever's commitment to rigorous research continued to shape OpenAI's trajectory.

The founding members' diverse backgrounds, united by a common goal, laid the foundation for OpenAI's unique position in the AI community. Their collective vision, articulated in the OpenAI Charter, became a guiding light for the organization as it navigated the uncharted waters of AGI development, leaving an indelible mark on the history of artificial intelligence.

Chapter 2: Exploring the Genesis of OpenAI and Addressing AI Risks

The creation of OpenAI emerged from a confluence of visionary foresight, technological optimism, and a profound sense of responsibility. This chapter delves into the motivations behind the establishment of OpenAI, examining the concerns about the potential risks of artificial intelligence (AI) that propelled its founding members, including Elon Musk, Sam Altman, Greg Brockman, Ilya Sutskever, and others, to embark on a mission to guide the development of AI for the benefit of humanity.

In the early 2010s, the field of artificial intelligence witnessed unprecedented advancements. Breakthroughs in machine learning, particularly in the domain of deep learning, had led to remarkable progress in tasks such as image recognition, natural language processing, and game-playing. AI systems, fueled by vast amounts of data and powerful computational resources, demonstrated capabilities that were previously considered the realm of science fiction.

These advancements fueled a wave of excitement and optimism about the transformative potential of AI. Industries saw the promise of increased efficiency, innovation, and new frontiers in problem-solving. However, amidst the enthusiasm, a growing awareness emerged about the potential risks associated with the unchecked development and deployment of increasingly powerful AI systems.

The Birth of OpenAI

Elon Musk's Warnings and Proactive Stance

A central figure in the establishment of OpenAI, Elon Musk, had been a vocal advocate for responsible AI development. Musk's public statements consistently underscored his concerns about the potential risks and unintended consequences of artificial general intelligence (AGI)—a level of AI that surpasses human intelligence across a broad range of tasks. In various interviews and forums, Musk expressed his apprehension that if AGI were not developed with adequate safety precautions, it could pose existential risks to humanity.

Musk's warnings were not mere speculative caution; they were a call to action. He believed that the development of AGI required a proactive and concerted effort to ensure its benefits were widely distributed and that its deployment did not inadvertently lead to harm. This proactive stance laid the foundation for the creation of OpenAI.

Shaping the Narrative: AGI as a Global Benefit

The motivation behind OpenAI was not solely driven by fear or alarm. Rather, it was rooted in a desire to shape the narrative around AGI as a global benefit. Musk, along with the other founding members, recognized the transformative potential of AGI in addressing some of humanity's most pressing challenges—from healthcare to climate change. The goal was to harness this potential in a manner that prioritized safety, ethical considerations, and equitable access. OpenAI, from its inception, was envisioned as a research organization committed to providing public goods. The term "public goods" in this context refers to resources that benefit society as a whole. In the case of OpenAI, this meant conducting research to make AGI safe and promoting the broad distribution of its benefits.

Concerns about AGI Risks

The concerns about AGI risks were rooted in the recognition that once AGI surpassed human intelligence, it would wield unprecedented power. This power, if not carefully managed, could lead to unintended consequences. The notion of an autonomous system with superhuman intelligence raised questions about its potential impact on economic systems, governance structures, and even the fabric of society.

The unpredictability of AGI behavior was a core concern. As AI systems became increasingly complex and autonomous, the ability to predict their actions with certainty diminished. This lack of predictability introduced the possibility of unintended and potentially adverse outcomes, amplifying the need for robust safety measures.

Centralization of Power

Another concern was the potential for the centralization of power in the hands of a few entities with advanced AGI capabilities. The fear was that organizations or individuals who controlled highly capable AI systems could wield disproportionate influence over global affairs. This concentration of power raised ethical, political, and socioeconomic questions, pointing to the need for mechanisms to prevent undue concentration of influence.

Strategic Considerations: Competitive Races and Global Cooperation

The competitive nature of technology development, especially in the context of AGI, added an additional layer of concern. The race to develop AGI could potentially lead to a scenario where safety precautions were sacrificed in the pursuit of technological milestones. The concept of an AGI development race underscored the need for a cooperative and collaborative approach to ensure that safety considerations were not compromised in the quest for technological supremacy.

OpenAI's concerns about AGI risks were not solely focused on immediate threats but also took a long-term perspective. The organization recognized that addressing AGI's challenges required foresight, strategic planning, and a commitment to mitigating risks well in advance of AGI becoming a reality.

OpenAI's Mission as a Response to Concerns

To address these concerns and motivations, OpenAI crafted its mission and principles, encapsulated in the OpenAI Charter. The Charter serves as a guiding document that outlines the organization's commitment to AGI safety, broad benefits, technical leadership, and cooperative orientation. The emphasis on AGI safety is a cornerstone of OpenAI's mission. The organization commits to conducting research to make AGI safe and driving the adoption of safety measures across the AI community. This proactive approach reflects OpenAI's acknowledgment of the need to address safety concerns throughout AGI development, minimizing the risks associated with its deployment.

Broadly Distributed Benefits

OpenAI's commitment to using any influence it obtains over AGI's deployment to ensure it benefits all of humanity underscores a dedication to avoiding the concentration of power. The organization envisions that access to, benefits from, and influence over AGI should be widespread, and it actively cooperates with other research and policy institutions to create a global community working together to address AGI's challenges.

Technical Leadership Aligned with Ethical Considerations

Balancing technical leadership with ethical considerations is a delicate task, and OpenAI's Charter explicitly addresses this challenge. The organization aims to be at the forefront of AI capabilities to effectively address AGI's impact on society. However, this pursuit is guided by a commitment to ensuring that the benefits are used for the collective good and that AGI is developed and deployed responsibly.

Cooperative Orientation

OpenAI recognizes the global nature of AGI's challenges and the need for a cooperative orientation. The organization actively seeks cooperation with other research and policy institutions, fostering a collaborative approach to address AGI's global challenges. This commitment to cooperation reflects a broader recognition that the responsible development and deployment of AGI require collective efforts and shared knowledge.

Navigating Challenges and Evolving Perspectives

As OpenAI embarked on its mission, the organization encountered the dynamic and rapidly evolving nature of AI development. The challenges posed by AGI's risks were not static; they evolved with advancements in technology, changes in the AI landscape, and the emergence of new ethical and societal considerations.

In response to these dynamics, OpenAI demonstrated an adaptive approach by updating its Charter. Charter updates reflected a commitment to continuous improvement, responsiveness to external input, and a willingness to iterate on principles based on evolving insights. This adaptability showcased OpenAI's dedication to refining its strategies to address the challenges of AGI development effectively.

An ongoing challenge for OpenAI has been striking the right balance between transparency and security. While transparency is essential for accountability and public understanding, considerations of security and avoiding unintended risks necessitate certain boundaries on disclosure. OpenAI's approach to navigating this delicate balance reflects an ongoing commitment to responsible and measured progress.

Funding Rounds and Financial Backing

The realization of OpenAI's ambitious mission required substantial financial backing. In the early years, the organization secured initial commitments from its founding members, with Elon Musk pledging a significant amount to kickstart OpenAI's operations. The financial support from Musk and others provided OpenAI with the autonomy and resources needed to pursue its mission without being beholden to short-term commercial interests.

While financial support was crucial, OpenAI adopted a cautious approach to funding, recognizing the potential for conflicts of interest that could arise from certain funding sources. The organization's commitment to AGI safety and broad benefit guided its decisions regarding funding partners. OpenAI aimed to avoid situations where short-term interests or specific agendas could compromise the long-term goals of ensuring AGI's safe and beneficial development.

As OpenAI expanded its scope and ambition, the organization recognized the need for substantial and diverse funding to address the scale and complexity of AGI development. This realization led to a strategic shift in OpenAI's approach to funding. In 2019, OpenAI announced a shift to a more cooperative orientation, seeking external investment to attract a wider range of contributors.

In 2019, OpenAI entered into a strategic partnership with Microsoft. The partnership involved a substantial investment from Microsoft, providing OpenAI with both financial resources and access to Microsoft's vast cloud computing infrastructure. This collaboration allowed OpenAI to leverage Microsoft's expertise and resources while maintaining its independence and commitment to its mission.

The external investment marked a significant milestone in OpenAI's funding history, showcasing a pragmatic approach to securing the necessary resources for its ambitious research agenda. The partnership with Microsoft demonstrated a balance between financial sustainability and maintaining OpenAI's mission-driven focus. The evolution of OpenAI's funding models reflected the organization's adaptability and commitment to its mission. The cautious approach to funding, the shift towards external investments, and strategic partnerships showcased a nuanced understanding of the challenges and opportunities associated with AGI development.

Legacy of the Early Years

The early years of OpenAI left an indelible mark on the AI landscape. The organization's commitment to transparency, safety, and collaborative research influenced the broader AI community. OpenAI's open-source contributions, research publications, and cooperative orientation set a precedent for responsible AI development.

OpenAI's early focus on fundamental research and technical leadership laid the groundwork for subsequent advancements in AI capabilities. The organization's exploration of deep learning, reinforcement learning, and natural language processing contributed to the scientific understanding of these domains, paving the way for future breakthroughs.

The careful balance between autonomy and external collaboration demonstrated in OpenAI's funding strategies became a model for other organizations navigating the complexities of AI development. The partnership with Microsoft showcased how strategic collaborations could provide financial support without compromising mission-driven goals.

Chapter 3: Research Focus - OpenAI's Exploration of Early Projects and Key Technologies

The heartbeat of OpenAI lies in its commitment to advancing the field of artificial intelligence (AI) through rigorous research and the development of cutting-edge technologies. This chapter delves into OpenAI's early years, exploring the organization's research focus, key projects, and the evolution of technologies that played a pivotal role in shaping the landscape of AI. From fundamental research to the deployment of practical applications, OpenAI's journey through its early projects showcases its dedication to technical leadership and innovation.

Foundational Research Areas

At the core of OpenAI's early research initiatives was a focus on deep learning—an approach that involves training artificial neural networks with multiple layers to perform complex tasks. The organization actively contributed to the advancement of deep learning techniques, exploring novel architectures, optimization methods, and applications across various domains.

One notable example of OpenAI's deep learning contributions was its work on reinforcement learning. The organization sought to enhance the capabilities of AI systems to learn and make decisions by interacting with their environment. OpenAI's research in this area aimed to push the boundaries of what AI could achieve in terms of decision-making, strategic planning, and autonomous learning.

OpenAI also delved into the realm of natural language processing (NLP), a field focused on enabling machines to understand, interpret, and generate human-like language. The organization's research in NLP aimed to develop models capable of understanding context, generating coherent text, and performing language-related tasks with a level of sophistication previously unseen.

Key projects in NLP included the development of language models that could generate contextually relevant and coherent sentences. OpenAI's work in this area contributed to advancements in language understanding, machine translation, and the generation of human-like text.

Early Projects

OpenAI Gym

In its commitment to advancing reinforcement learning research, OpenAI introduced OpenAI Gym—a toolkit for developing and comparing reinforcement learning algorithms. OpenAI Gym provided a standardized environment for researchers and developers to test and benchmark their algorithms across a range of tasks, from simple games to more complex scenarios.

The release of OpenAI Gym marked a significant contribution to the AI community, fostering collaboration and accelerating progress in reinforcement learning research. The toolkit became a widely used platform for researchers to evaluate and compare the performance of their algorithms, contributing to the collective understanding of reinforcement learning methods.

GPT-2: Language Model Advancements

One of the landmark projects in OpenAI's early years was the development of the Generative Pre-trained Transformer 2 (GPT-2). GPT-2 represented a breakthrough in natural language processing, demonstrating the capabilities of large-scale language models. The model, pre-trained on a diverse range of internet text, exhibited remarkable proficiency in generating coherent and contextually relevant text across a wide array of topics.

The release of GPT-2 generated widespread attention and discussions regarding the ethical implications of powerful language models. OpenAI's decision to initially withhold the full model due to concerns about potential misuse underscored the organization's commitment to responsible AI development.

Robotics and Physical Interaction

Beyond virtual environments, OpenAI ventured into the realm of physical interaction and robotics. The organization explored the application of reinforcement learning to robotic systems, aiming to enable machines to learn complex motor skills and manipulation tasks. OpenAI's research in this domain sought to bridge the gap between virtual simulations and the physical world, advancing the capabilities of AI systems in real-world scenarios.

Technical Leadership and Innovation

OpenAI's early projects were characterized by a commitment to pushing the boundaries of AI capabilities. The organization actively pursued research questions and technical challenges that demanded innovation and creative problem-solving. Whether in the domain of language understanding, reinforcement learning, or robotics, OpenAI's projects were at the forefront of AI research, contributing to the state-of-the-art in multiple fields.

A distinctive feature of OpenAI's research approach was its exploration of large-scale models. The organization recognized the impact of model scale on the performance of AI systems and actively engaged in developing models with unprecedented size and complexity. This approach, exemplified by projects like GPT-2, demonstrated OpenAI's dedication to technical leadership by consistently pushing the envelope in terms of model size and capabilities. In addition to advancements in AI capabilities, OpenAI actively researched topics related to safety and robustness. The organization acknowledged the potential risks associated with powerful AI systems and sought to address these concerns through dedicated research initiatives. This dual focus on technical innovation and safety considerations reflected OpenAI's commitment to responsible AI development.

Challenges and Ethical Considerations

Ethical Implications of Large Language Models

The development of large language models, such as GPT-2, raised important ethical considerations. The potential for misuse, misinformation, and the generation of harmful content prompted OpenAI to carefully consider the responsible release of such models. The organization's decision to initially limit access to the full GPT-2 model highlighted the ethical considerations associated with deploying powerful language models into the public domain.

Balancing Technical Innovation with Safety

OpenAI navigated the delicate balance between technical innovation and safety. The pursuit of cutting-edge research in AI capabilities required a nuanced approach to safety considerations. The organization actively engaged in research to make AI systems safe and robust, acknowledging the need to address potential risks associated with the deployment of advanced technologies.

Collaborative Initiatives

OpenAI's Commitment to Collaboration

OpenAI's early years were marked by a commitment to collaboration and knowledge sharing. The organization actively sought partnerships with other research institutions, industry collaborators, and the broader AI community. OpenAI recognized that addressing the complex challenges of AI development required a collaborative and cooperative approach.

Participation in AI Competitions

As part of its collaborative initiatives, OpenAI participated in various AI competitions. The organization's involvement in competitions served multiple purposes—it provided a platform to benchmark the performance of its models, facilitated collaboration with the broader research community, and contributed to the advancement of AI research through friendly competition.

Evolution of Key Technologies

GPT-3: Scaling Language Models

Building upon the success of GPT-2, OpenAI continued to scale language models with the release of Generative Pre-trained Transformer 3 (GPT-3). GPT-3 represented a significant leap in model size and complexity, with 175 billion parameters. The model demonstrated unprecedented capabilities in natural language understanding, generation, and performing a wide range of language-related tasks.

The release of GPT-3 showcased OpenAI's ongoing commitment to advancing key technologies, pushing the boundaries of what AI systems could achieve. The model's versatility and proficiency in various language tasks highlighted the evolution of language models as a key technological frontier.

Reinforcement Learning Advancements

OpenAI's exploration of reinforcement learning continued to evolve, with advancements in algorithms and techniques. The organization sought to enhance the efficiency and effectiveness of reinforcement learning methods, enabling AI systems to learn and adapt more rapidly in dynamic environments. These advancements in reinforcement learning contributed to the broader landscape of AI research and applications.

Continued Focus on Safety and Ethical AI

As OpenAI scaled its research efforts and explored new frontiers, the organization maintained a steadfast commitment to safety and ethical AI. Research initiatives addressing the interpretability of AI models, the mitigation of biases, and the development of frameworks for safe deployment underscored OpenAI's dedication to responsible and inclusive AI development.

Chapter 4: Key Milestones - AlphaGo Match: OpenAI's Reaction and Research Impact

Key milestones in OpenAI's journey not only mark significant achievements but also serve as critical junctures that shape the organization's trajectory. One such pivotal moment was the series of victories by AlphaGo, Google DeepMind's Go-playing AI, against human world champions. This chapter explores OpenAI's reaction to the AlphaGo victories and delves into the impact these events had on OpenAI's research agenda and strategic considerations.

AlphaGo: A Watershed Moment in AI

In 2016, AlphaGo, developed by DeepMind, achieved an unprecedented level of success by defeating Lee Sedol, a world champion Go player, in a five-game match. This victory marked a watershed moment in the field of artificial intelligence, demonstrating the capacity of AI systems to master complex, intuitive games that were previously considered uniquely human. AlphaGo's success was underpinned by advancements in deep learning and reinforcement learning. The combination of neural network architectures, Monte Carlo tree search algorithms, and powerful computational resources enabled AlphaGo to surpass human expertise in the ancient and highly intricate game of Go.

The victories of AlphaGo garnered global attention and sparked conversations within the AI community about the potential and implications of advanced AI systems. OpenAI, as a prominent research organization, recognized the significance of AlphaGo's achievements and the transformative potential of deep learning techniques. The success of AlphaGo prompted OpenAI to reflect on the pace of AI advancements. The rapid progression from traditional approaches to AI, which struggled with the complexities of Go, to the breakthroughs achieved by AlphaGo signaled an acceleration in the capabilities of AI systems. This prompted OpenAI to assess the implications of such advancements for its own research agenda and the broader landscape of AI development.

Impact on OpenAI's Research Agenda

The AlphaGo victories underscored the potential of deep learning techniques in conquering complex problems. OpenAI, already engaged in cutting-edge research, recognized that advancements in deep learning could have far-reaching implications for the organization's own research agenda. The success of AlphaGo served as a catalyst for OpenAI to explore new possibilities and directions within the realm of AI. The success of AlphaGo highlighted the effectiveness of reinforcement learning in achieving superhuman performance in strategic games. OpenAI, with its focus on reinforcement learning, took inspiration from AlphaGo's accomplishments. The organization saw an opportunity to deepen its understanding of reinforcement learning algorithms and their applications, aiming to contribute to the growing body of knowledge in this domain. The AlphaGo victories reinforced the importance of technical excellence in AI research. OpenAI recognized that achieving breakthroughs in complex tasks required not only innovative approaches but also a commitment to pushing the boundaries of what AI systems could accomplish. This realization influenced OpenAI's research culture, placing a heightened emphasis on technical rigor and excellence.

Evolving Landscape of AI Development

The success of AlphaGo contributed to a shift in the perception of what AI systems could achieve. The rapid progress demonstrated by AlphaGo suggested that certain benchmarks, once considered distant, were within reach. OpenAI acknowledged the evolving landscape of AI development and the need to continually reassess its strategies in response to the dynamic nature of the field. The achievements of AlphaGo prompted OpenAI to strike a balance between ambition and realism in its own research goals. While aiming for groundbreaking advancements, OpenAI recognized the importance of setting realistic expectations and aligning its objectives with the current state of AI capabilities. This strategic recalibration influenced how OpenAI framed its mission and the milestones it sought to achieve.

OpenAI embraced the iterative nature of research, recognizing that breakthroughs often come through a process of continuous learning and refinement. The organization absorbed lessons from AlphaGo's success, incorporating insights into its own research methodologies. This iterative approach became a hallmark of OpenAI's pursuit of technical excellence and innovation. The success of AlphaGo emphasized the importance of cross-disciplinary collaboration. OpenAI recognized that advancements in AI required expertise from diverse fields, including computer science, mathematics, and neuroscience. The organization fostered a collaborative culture that encouraged the exchange of ideas and insights across different disciplines, enriching its research endeavors. AlphaGo's victories also brought to the forefront ethical and societal implications associated with the rapid advancement of AI technologies. OpenAI, already committed to responsible AI development, incorporated lessons from AlphaGo's impact on public discourse. The organization reaffirmed its dedication to addressing ethical considerations, ensuring transparency, and actively engaging with the broader public in discussions about the societal impact of AI.

Leveraging Inspiration for Innovation

Rather than viewing AlphaGo's successes as a conclusion, OpenAI leveraged the inspiration derived from these victories to fuel its own pursuit of innovation. The organization sought to channel the momentum created by AlphaGo into its research initiatives, exploring novel ideas and methodologies that could contribute to the evolving landscape of AI development. OpenAI's commitment to providing public goods aligned with the ethos demonstrated by AlphaGo's developers. The organization continued to contribute to the open-source community, sharing research papers, code, and models. OpenAI recognized the importance of knowledge sharing in fostering a collaborative and transparent AI community, echoing the principles exemplified by the success of AlphaGo. The impact of AlphaGo prompted OpenAI to remain agile and adaptable in the face of new challenges. The organization recognized that the field of AI would continue to evolve, presenting novel obstacles and opportunities. OpenAI's ability to adapt to emerging trends and challenges became a defining characteristic of its ongoing research endeavors.

While AlphaGo showcased the potential of AI in strategic games, OpenAI acknowledged the need to expand its research horizons. The organization explored applications of AI in diverse domains, including natural language processing, robotics, and reinforcement learning for real-world scenarios. This expansion of research horizons reflected OpenAI's commitment to addressing a broad spectrum of challenges beyond specific benchmarks. The AlphaGo victories marked a seminal moment in the history of AI, prompting OpenAI to reflect, adapt, and innovate. The organization's reaction to AlphaGo's successes influenced its research agenda, strategic considerations, and organizational culture. OpenAI embraced the lessons learned from AlphaGo, incorporating them into its ongoing pursuit of technical excellence, responsible AI development, and collaborative engagement with the broader AI community.

As OpenAI navigated the dynamic landscape of AI research, the impact of AlphaGo continued to resonate, serving as a touchstone for the organization's commitment to pushing the boundaries of what AI systems could achieve while remaining mindful of the ethical and societal implications of advanced technologies. The legacy of AlphaGo's victories became woven into the fabric of OpenAI's journey, shaping its mission, values, and ongoing contributions to the field of artificial intelligence.

Chapter 5: GPT Series - Evolution of the Generative Pre-trained Transformer

The Generative Pre-trained Transformer (GPT) series demonstrates OpenAI's dedication to enhancing natural language processing and generating capabilities. This chapter delves into the progress and milestones of the GPT series, from GPT-1 to GPT-3. Built on transformer architecture and pre-trained on enormous datasets, these models have transformed the landscape of language interpretation and creation, demonstrating OpenAI's commitment to technical quality and innovation.

GPT-1: Inaugurating a New Era

The GPT series began with the release of GPT-1 in June 2018. GPT-1, which was built on transformer architecture, proved the power of large-scale language models that had been pre-trained on varied datasets. The model has 117 million parameters, which allowed it to detect detailed patterns and correlations in the data. Pre-training for GPT-1 included exposure to a wide range of online material, allowing the model to grasp the complexities of language, syntax, and context. Following pre-training, the model's skills were fine-tuned on particular tasks, making it amenable to a variety of applications such as text completion, question answering, and language translation. GPT-1 advanced significantly in natural language understanding. The model demonstrated the ability to create coherent and contextually appropriate text, demonstrating advances in language modeling. GPT-1's performance laid the groundwork for following iterations in the GPT series, establishing a precedent for large-scale, pre-trained language models.

GPT-2: Scaling New Heights

GPT-2, unveiled in February 2019, marked a monumental leap in both model size and complexity. With a staggering 1.5 billion parameters, GPT-2 dwarfed its predecessor, enabling it to capture intricate details and nuances in language with unparalleled fidelity. The release of GPT-2 sparked widespread attention and raised concerns about the potential misuse of powerful language models. In response, OpenAI initially chose to withhold the full model, releasing only smaller versions. This cautious approach demonstrated OpenAI's commitment to responsible AI development and its acknowledgment of the ethical considerations associated with advanced language models. GPT-2 showcased remarkable capabilities in creative text generation. The model could generate coherent and contextually relevant text across diverse prompts, ranging from news articles to fictional storytelling. The creativity exhibited by GPT-2 sparked conversations about the potential impact of advanced language models on content creation and storytelling. GPT-2's success contributed to OpenAI's mission of advancing artificial general intelligence (AGI) while emphasizing the importance of safety and responsible deployment. The model's ability to understand and generate human-like text exemplified the transformative potential of large-scale language models in various applications.

GPT-3: Pushing the Boundaries

GPT-3, introduced in June 2020, emerged as a groundbreaking model in terms of scale and complexity. With a staggering 175 billion parameters, GPT-3 represented a quantum leap in the size of language models. The sheer scale of GPT-3 allowed it to exhibit unparalleled proficiency in natural language understanding and generation. One of GPT-3's defining features was its versatility. The model demonstrated the ability to perform a wide array of language-related tasks without task-specific training. The concept of zero-shot learning—where the model could generalize across tasks without explicit training for each—showcased GPT-3's adaptability and hinted at the potential for more generalized language understanding. GPT-3's capabilities found applications across diverse domains. From content creation and code generation to language translation and question answering, the model showcased its versatility in understanding and generating text in ways that surpassed its predecessors. GPT-3's impact reverberated across industries, offering a glimpse into the transformative potential of large-scale language models.

As GPT-3 garnered attention, OpenAI remained mindful of the ethical and societal implications associated with its deployment. The organization actively engaged in discussions about responsible AI development, transparency, and the potential biases inherent in large language models. GPT-3's prominence intensified the discourse on the responsible use of advanced AI technologies.

The Evolution of GPT Series: Milestones and Contributions

The GPT series, from GPT-1 to GPT-3, exemplified a continuous advancement in language modeling. The models demonstrated an increasing proficiency in understanding context, generating coherent text, and performing diverse language-related tasks. The evolution of the GPT series showcased OpenAI's dedication to pushing the boundaries of what language models could achieve. The GPT series left an indelible mark on both AI research and industry applications. Researchers leveraged the pre-trained models for downstream tasks, accelerating progress in natural language processing. In industry settings, the GPT series found applications in content generation, customer support, and various language-related tasks, showcasing the practical implications of large language models. A consistent theme across the GPT series was OpenAI's commitment to providing public goods. The organization actively shared research papers, code, and models, contributing to the open-source community and fostering collaboration. This commitment aligned with OpenAI's mission of ensuring that the benefits of AI were broadly distributed for the betterment of humanity.

Ethical Considerations and Mitigation Strategies

As the GPT series gained prominence, OpenAI proactively addressed ethical considerations associated with large language models. The organization invested in research to understand and mitigate biases, engaged in conversations about responsible AI use, and sought external input to shape its practices. The emphasis on ethical considerations reflected OpenAI's commitment to the responsible deployment of advanced AI technologies. The development of the GPT series underscored the iterative nature of model development. Each iteration built upon the successes and challenges of its predecessors, demonstrating OpenAI's capacity for continuous learning and improvement. The GPT series served as a testament to the dynamic and evolving nature of AI research. The GPT series highlighted the delicate balance between model scale and responsible deployment. While larger models exhibited unprecedented capabilities, concerns about potential biases, misuse, and ethical implications necessitated careful considerations in deployment strategies. OpenAI's approach to responsible release showcased a nuanced understanding of the challenges associated with deploying advanced language models. The societal impact of the GPT series prompted OpenAI to actively engage with the public. The organization sought external input, encouraged discussions on ethical AI development, and embraced transparency in sharing its research findings. The public engagement initiatives reflected OpenAI's commitment to inclusivity and the recognition that the societal impact of AI extended beyond technical considerations.

Legacy of the GPT Series

- The GPT series, with its unprecedented scale and capabilities, played a pivotal role in shaping the landscape of natural language processing. The models set new benchmarks for language understanding, generation, and versatility. The GPT series became reference points for researchers, practitioners, and the broader AI community, influencing the trajectory of language model development. The GPT series left a lasting legacy in emphasizing responsible AI development. OpenAI's proactive approach to addressing ethical considerations, mitigating biases, and engaging with the public became a guiding principle for the organization and influenced broader conversations about the responsible use of AI technologies. The GPT series served as a catalyst for further innovation in natural language processing. Researchers and organizations leveraged the insights gained from the GPT models to explore new frontiers in AI, from understanding complex language nuances to developing applications that could revolutionize industries. The GPT series's impact extended beyond its immediate applications, inspiring a new wave of creativity and exploration in the AI community. The GPT series, from GPT-1 to GPT-3, represents a remarkable journey in the evolution of large-scale language models. OpenAI's commitment to technical excellence, responsible AI development, and public goods is evident throughout the series. The models' impact on natural language processing, research practices, and industry applications underscores the transformative potential of advanced language models. As the GPT series continues to influence the field of artificial intelligence, OpenAI remains at the forefront of innovation, navigating the complexities of model development, addressing ethical considerations, and contributing to the collective knowledge of the AI community. The legacy of the GPT series is not just in the models themselves but in the principles they embody—principles that guide OpenAI's mission to ensure that artificial general intelligence benefits all of humanity.

Chapter 6: Industry Collaborations - OpenAI's Partnerships and Research Endeavors

OpenAI's journey in the field of artificial intelligence (AI) has been marked not only by its internal research endeavors but also by strategic collaborations with industry partners and research institutions. This chapter delves into the landscape of OpenAI's industry collaborations, examining the motivations behind these partnerships, the key players involved, and the impact on the broader AI ecosystem. One of the primary motivations behind OpenAI's industry collaborations is the shared goal of advancing AI research and development. Collaborating with industry partners provides OpenAI with access to diverse perspectives, expertise, and resources. This collective effort accelerates progress in the field, fostering innovation and pushing the boundaries of what AI systems can achieve. Industry collaborations allow OpenAI to tap into complementary expertise that may not be present within the organization. By partnering with companies and research institutions specializing in specific domains or technologies, OpenAI can leverage synergies that enhance the depth and breadth of its research initiatives. Collaborations often involve resource sharing, including access to computational infrastructure, datasets, and specialized tools. This access to shared resources enables OpenAI to conduct experiments at a larger scale and facilitates the exploration of more ambitious research questions. Collaborative infrastructure also promotes efficiency and cost-effectiveness in AI research.

Key Industry Collaborations

One of OpenAI's notable industry collaborations is its partnership with Microsoft. In 2019, OpenAI and Microsoft announced a strategic collaboration focused on jointly developing artificial general intelligence (AGI). The partnership aimed to leverage Microsoft's expertise in cloud computing and OpenAI's research capabilities to address the challenges associated with AGI development.

The collaboration involved OpenAI using Microsoft Azure as its primary cloud provider, allowing OpenAI to benefit from

Azure's scalable infrastructure. The partnership exemplified the importance of industry collaboration in addressing the complex and resource-intensive nature of AGI research.

OpenAI's ties with Tesla, a company co-founded by Elon Musk, one of OpenAI's original founders, have also been notable. While not a conventional collaboration, the affiliation has facilitated a flow of ideas and insights between OpenAI and Tesla, contributing to the exchange of knowledge in the broader field of AI and autonomous systems.

The intersection of AI and autonomous vehicles represents a domain where OpenAI's research on reinforcement learning and machine perception aligns with Tesla's endeavors. Although the collaboration is indirect, the exchange of expertise underscores the interconnectedness of AI research and industry applications.

Beyond industry partnerships, OpenAI actively collaborates with research institutions to foster academic contributions and collaborations. These collaborations serve as a bridge between industry and academia, promoting the exchange of ideas and the advancement of fundamental AI research. OpenAI's collaborations with institutions such as Stanford University, Massachusetts Institute of Technology (MIT), and others provide a platform for joint research projects, workshops, and knowledge sharing. These partnerships contribute to the academic community's understanding of AI and its applications.

Impact on AI Research

Industry collaborations have played a pivotal role in accelerating the progress of AI capabilities. By partnering with companies at the forefront of technological innovation, OpenAI gains insights into real-world challenges and cutting-edge developments. This direct exposure to industry needs informs OpenAI's research agenda, guiding the organization to address practical applications and contribute to the advancement of AI technologies. The cross-pollination of ideas between OpenAI and its industry collaborators fosters a dynamic exchange of insights. As researchers from different backgrounds and industries come together, they bring diverse perspectives, methodologies, and approaches to problem-solving. This diversity of thought enriches the research landscape, leading to more robust and comprehensive solutions.

Collaborating with industry partners provides OpenAI with opportunities to validate its research findings in real-world scenarios. Implementing AI solutions in collaboration with companies allows OpenAI to assess the effectiveness and practicality of its models and algorithms. This validation loop is crucial for refining research outcomes and ensuring their relevance to industry applications.

Challenges and Considerations

Balancing Autonomy and Collaborative Goals

One of the challenges in industry collaborations is striking the right balance between OpenAI's autonomy in research and the collaborative goals of the partnership. While collaborations aim to harness collective expertise, OpenAI remains committed to its mission of ensuring that artificial general intelligence benefits all of humanity. Navigating the dynamics of collaboration while maintaining the organization's core principles requires careful consideration.

Addressing Ethical and Societal Implications

Industry collaborations raise ethical considerations, especially when deploying AI technologies with potential societal impact. OpenAI is mindful of the ethical implications associated with the use of its models and algorithms in real-world applications. Collaborative efforts involve discussions on responsible AI development, transparency, and the need to mitigate biases to ensure that AI benefits society at large.

Managing Intellectual Property and Knowledge Sharing

Collaborations often involve the exchange of intellectual property and knowledge. Managing this exchange requires clear agreements on intellectual property rights, data sharing, and publication policies. Striking a balance between sharing knowledge for the collective benefit and protecting proprietary information is a complex aspect of industry collaborations that OpenAI navigates to ensure the responsible dissemination of research outcomes.

Collaborative Initiatives and Contributions

Industry collaborations manifest in joint research projects that address specific challenges and opportunities. These projects often result in published papers, open-source contributions, and advancements in AI research. Joint efforts with industry partners amplify the impact of research findings, making them accessible to the broader scientific community.

Workshops and Conferences

OpenAI actively participates in and organizes workshops and conferences in collaboration with industry partners and research institutions. These events serve as platforms for knowledge exchange, showcasing the latest advancements, and fostering discussions on emerging trends and challenges in AI research.

Contribution to Open Source

OpenAI's commitment to public goods extends to its collaborative initiatives. The organization actively contributes to the open-source community by sharing research papers, code, and models resulting from collaborative projects. This commitment to openness promotes transparency and knowledge dissemination, benefiting researchers and practitioners in the wider AI community.

Evolving Landscape and Future Directions

The landscape of AI research and development is dynamic, with emerging technologies continually shaping the field. OpenAI's industry collaborations position the organization to adapt to these changes and stay at the forefront of technological advancements. The adaptability to emerging technologies ensures that OpenAI remains agile in addressing new challenges and opportunities. As industry collaborations evolve, OpenAI maintains a steadfast commitment to responsible AI development. The organization actively engages in conversations about ethical considerations, potential biases, and societal impact. OpenAI's dedication to responsible AI aligns with its mission to ensure that the benefits of artificial general intelligence are broadly distributed for the well-being of humanity.

Collaborations with industry partners serve as catalysts for innovation, propelling the field of AI forward. By fostering an environment of collaboration, OpenAI not only contributes to advancements in research but also inspires new ideas and approaches. The collective intelligence generated through collaborations has the potential to drive breakthroughs that may not be achievable through individual efforts alone. OpenAI's industry collaborations stand as integral components of its broader mission to advance artificial general intelligence for the benefit of humanity. These collaborations provide avenues for knowledge exchange, resource sharing, and the application of AI research in real-world scenarios. As the field of AI continues to evolve, OpenAI's commitment to industry partnerships, responsible AI development, and the open dissemination of knowledge remains pivotal in shaping the trajectory of AI research and its impact on society.

The Philosophy of Open Source at OpenAI

OpenAI's commitment to open source aligns with the philosophy of democratizing AI knowledge. By making research findings, models, and code publicly accessible, OpenAI empowers researchers, developers, and the broader community to build upon and contribute to the collective body of AI knowledge. This ethos reflects a commitment to inclusivity and the belief that AI advancements should be widely shared. Open source serves as an accelerator for research progress. By releasing models and code, OpenAI enables the broader AI community to replicate, refine, and extend its work. This collaborative approach fosters a culture of innovation, where researchers across the globe can leverage and build upon each other's contributions, leading to faster advancements in the field. OpenAI's commitment to open source is intertwined with its dedication to ethical and responsible AI development. Transparency in sharing research findings and code promotes accountability, allowing the community to scrutinize and assess the implications of AI models. This commitment is rooted in OpenAI's mission to ensure that AGI benefits all of humanity.

Releases of Various AI Models

The release of the Generative Pre-trained Transformer (GPT) series exemplifies OpenAI's commitment to sharing cutting-edge AI models with the world. GPT-1, GPT-2, and GPT-3 have all been released, accompanied by research papers, code, and pre-trained models.

These releases not only showcase advancements in natural language processing but also provide valuable resources for researchers and developers to explore and integrate large-scale language models into their projects.

OpenAI Baselines

OpenAI Baselines is a collection of high-quality implementations of reinforcement learning algorithms. Released as open-source projects, these baselines provide a benchmark for researchers and developers working on reinforcement learning tasks. The availability of well-documented, tested, and extensible code facilitates the reproducibility of results and accelerates progress in reinforcement learning research.

Spinning Up in Deep Learning

"Spinning Up in Deep Learning" is an educational resource released by OpenAI. It provides a practical and accessible guide to deep learning, offering introductory material, tutorials, and code examples. This open-source initiative aims to lower the barriers to entry for individuals interested in deep learning, fostering a more inclusive and diverse community of practitioners.

Gym: A Toolkit for Developing and Comparing Reinforcement Learning Algorithms

OpenAI Gym is an open-source toolkit for developing and comparing reinforcement learning algorithms. It provides a standardized environment for testing and benchmarking RL algorithms, making it easier for researchers and developers to evaluate and compare the performance of their models. OpenAI Gym has become a widely used resource in the reinforcement learning community.

Impact on the AI Community

OpenAI's open-source contributions have fostered collaboration and innovation within the AI community. By sharing models, code, and educational resources, OpenAI empowers researchers and developers to collaborate on shared challenges, leading to novel solutions and breakthroughs. This collaborative spirit accelerates the pace of innovation in AI.

The release of state-of-the-art models like GPT-3 as open source has democratized access to cutting-edge AI capabilities. Researchers and developers around the world can explore, experiment, and integrate these models into their applications, irrespective of their institutional affiliations or resources. This democratization of access promotes a more equitable distribution of AI capabilities.

OpenAI's open-source initiatives, such as "Spinning Up in Deep Learning" and OpenAI Gym, contribute to the advancement of education and skill development in AI. These resources provide a valuable learning path for individuals looking to enter the field, offering practical guidance, hands-on examples, and benchmarks for aspiring researchers and practitioners.

Ethical Use and Responsible AI

OpenAI's commitment to open source raises considerations regarding the ethical use and responsible deployment of AI models. The accessibility of powerful models like GPT-3 to the broader community necessitates a careful balance between promoting innovation and ensuring that the technology is used responsibly. OpenAI actively addresses these considerations through guidelines, engagement with the community, and ongoing research. The release of AI models, particularly those trained on large and diverse datasets, comes with the responsibility to mitigate potential biases. OpenAI acknowledges the importance of addressing biases and actively works on research and development efforts to enhance the fairness and inclusivity of its models. The organization encourages the community to provide feedback and insights to collectively improve model performance. OpenAI faces the challenge of balancing transparency in research with considerations related to intellectual property. While open source promotes transparency, certain aspects of research and development may involve proprietary information. Striking the right balance ensures that OpenAI can share knowledge responsibly while protecting its capacity for innovation.

Future Directions and Continuous Innovation

OpenAI's commitment to open source is expected to evolve with the organization's ongoing research and development initiatives. Future releases may include advancements in natural language processing, reinforcement learning, and other areas of AI. The evolution of open-source initiatives will likely reflect the dynamic nature of the field and OpenAI's strategic priorities. As AI continues to advance, OpenAI's open-source contributions may extend into new challenges and domains. Emerging technologies, interdisciplinary research, and novel applications of AI could shape the direction of future open-source releases. OpenAI's adaptability to address new challenges ensures that its open-source initiatives remain relevant and impactful. OpenAI's open-source initiatives are expected to continue fostering community engagement and feedback. The organization values the insights and perspectives of the broader AI community, recognizing the collective intelligence that arises through collaborative efforts. Ongoing engagement ensures that open-source contributions reflect diverse perspectives and contribute to the mutual growth of the AI community.

OpenAI's commitment to open source is a fundamental aspect of its mission to ensure that the benefits of artificial general intelligence are broadly distributed. By releasing various AI models, code, and educational resources,

OpenAI empowers researchers, developers, and learners worldwide. The impact of open-source contributions extends beyond individual projects, fostering collaboration, democratizing access to cutting-edge technologies, and advancing the field of AI as a collective endeavor. As OpenAI continues to navigate the evolving landscape of AI, its dedication to open source remains a driving force for innovation and progress in artificial intelligence.

Chapter 7: Controversies, Long-Term Vision, and Reflections on OpenAI's Journey

Controversies and Criticisms

OpenAI's release of GPT-3, one of the most powerful language models to date, sparked debates and controversies surrounding access and use. While the model's capabilities were groundbreaking, concerns emerged about potential misuse, ethical considerations, and the environmental impact of training such large models. OpenAI addressed these concerns by carefully managing access to GPT-3 and emphasizing responsible AI use in its usage policies.

The issue of biases in language models gained prominence with the release of GPT-3. Critics argued that the model exhibited biases present in the training data, leading to potentially biased outputs. OpenAI acknowledged this concern and actively sought feedback to improve the model's behavior. The controversy underscored the broader challenge of addressing biases in AI models and prompted OpenAI to enhance its efforts in this regard.

The decision to initially withhold the full GPT-2 model raised eyebrows and ignited discussions about responsible disclosure in AI research. OpenAI expressed concerns about potential misuse, particularly in the generation of deceptive or malicious content. While the decision was motivated by a desire to act responsibly, it also stirred debates about the balance between transparency and control in the release of advanced AI models.

OpenAI's business model, which involves offering exclusive access and premium services to fund its research, drew both support and criticism. Some argued that this approach allowed OpenAI to sustain its ambitious research goals, while others expressed concerns about potential exclusivity and its implications for the broader research community. OpenAI addressed these concerns by maintaining a balance between exclusive access and providing public goods.

Long-Term Vision and Goals

OpenAI's long-term vision revolves around the development of artificial general intelligence (AGI) that benefits all of humanity. AGI, often referred to as highly autonomous systems that outperform humans at most economically valuable work, is seen as a transformative milestone in the field of AI. OpenAI envisions AGI with a high level of safety and broadly distributed benefits, and the organization is dedicated to conducting research to make AGI safe and promoting its broad adoption.

A key element of OpenAI's long-term vision is to be on the cutting edge of AI capabilities. By maintaining technical leadership, OpenAI aims to effectively address AGI's impact on society. This involves conducting advanced research, staying ahead of developments in the field, and actively contributing to the global AI community. Technical leadership is seen as a prerequisite for fulfilling OpenAI's mission to ensure the responsible and beneficial deployment of AGI.

OpenAI emphasizes a cooperative orientation in its approach to AGI development. The organization actively collaborates with other research and policy institutions, striving to create a global community that addresses the global challenges associated with AGI. The cooperative orientation is grounded in the recognition that AGI's impact transcends organizational and national boundaries, requiring collective efforts to navigate its complexities.

Broader Distribution of Benefits

Ensuring the broader distribution of benefits is a fundamental goal for OpenAI. The organization is committed to using any influence it obtains over AGI to ensure it is used for the benefit of all of humanity. OpenAI aims to avoid enabling uses of AI or AGI that could harm humanity or unduly concentrate power. The focus on broad benefits aligns with OpenAI's mission to minimize conflicts of interest and prioritize the well-being of humanity.

OpenAI envisions playing a role in AI's global policy and safety efforts. As AGI development progresses, the need for robust governance mechanisms becomes crucial. OpenAI commits to actively cooperating with other research and policy institutions to create a global community addressing AGI's challenges. The organization emphasizes the importance of avoiding AGI development becoming a competitive race without adequate safety precautions.

Reflections on OpenAI's Journey

OpenAI's journey reflects the dynamic evolution of the AI research landscape. From the early days, marked by foundational research and collaborations, to the development and release of state-of-the-art models like GPT-3, OpenAI has been a central player in shaping the trajectory of AI. The organization's contributions have influenced not only the field's technical aspects but also ethical considerations, responsible AI development, and the broader societal impact of AI.

One notable aspect of OpenAI's journey is its responsiveness to ethical concerns and criticisms. Controversies surrounding biases, responsible disclosure, and potential misuse prompted OpenAI to actively engage with the community, seek feedback, and iterate on its models and policies. This responsiveness reflects a commitment to ethical considerations, transparency, and a willingness to learn and adapt in the rapidly evolving landscape of AI research.

OpenAI's journey exemplifies the delicate balance between innovation and responsibility in AI development. The organization has consistently pushed the boundaries of what AI systems can achieve while actively addressing ethical, societal, and environmental considerations. The release of powerful models like GPT-3 has demonstrated OpenAI's commitment to advancing the state of the art, coupled with a responsible approach to their deployment.

OpenAI's commitment to open source and education has had a profound impact on the accessibility and inclusivity of AI knowledge. By releasing models, code, and educational resources, OpenAI has empowered researchers, developers, and learners worldwide. Initiatives like "Spinning Up in Deep Learning" and OpenAI Gym have contributed to the democratization of AI knowledge, fostering a more diverse and collaborative AI community.

OpenAI's journey is characterized by an ongoing commitment to learning and adaptability. The organization actively seeks external input, engages with the broader AI community, and embraces a culture of continuous improvement. This adaptability has been evident in OpenAI's responses to controversies, the evolution of its research priorities, and its initiatives to address emerging challenges in AI development.

Significance in the History of Artificial Intelligence

OpenAI's significance in the history of artificial intelligence lies in its role as a driving force behind the advancement of the state of the art. The GPT series, in particular, has set new benchmarks for natural language processing, demonstrating the potential of large-scale language models in understanding and generating human-like text. OpenAI's technical leadership has influenced the broader AI community and accelerated progress in AI capabilities.

OpenAI has been a pioneer in emphasizing responsible AI development. The organization's commitment to ethical considerations, transparency, and the responsible release of advanced models has set a standard for the industry. OpenAI's approach to addressing biases, mitigating potential misuse, and actively engaging with the public reflects a commitment to ensuring that AI technologies benefit humanity while minimizing risks.

OpenAI's dedication to open source and knowledge sharing has had a lasting impact on the democratization of AI knowledge. By releasing models, code, and educational resources, OpenAI has made cutting-edge AI capabilities accessible to a global audience. This commitment to openness has not only accelerated research progress but has also contributed to the growth and diversity of the AI community.

OpenAI's role in shaping conversations on AGI governance is a testament to its forward-looking approach. The organization actively engages with other research and policy institutions, emphasizing the need for cooperative efforts to address the global challenges associated with AGI. OpenAI's advocacy for robust governance mechanisms reflects a commitment to navigating the societal impact of AGI responsibly.

OpenAI's journey serves as an inspiration for future generations of researchers, developers, and AI enthusiasts. The organization's commitment to technical excellence, ethical considerations, and open collaboration sets a standard for the responsible and transformative development of AI. OpenAI's impact extends beyond its immediate contributions, inspiring a new wave of creativity and exploration in the AI community.

Conclusion

OpenAI's journey through controversies, long-term vision, and reflections on its significance in the history of artificial intelligence encapsulates a dynamic and evolving narrative. From the inception marked by visionary goals to the release of groundbreaking models and the active engagement with ethical considerations, OpenAI has played a central role in shaping the AI landscape.

As OpenAI continues its pursuit of artificial general intelligence, the organization remains steadfast in its commitment to technical leadership, responsible AI development, and the broader distribution of benefits. The significance of OpenAI extends beyond technical achievements to its impact on open source, education, and governance conversations surrounding AGI.

OpenAI's journey reflects the complex interplay between innovation and responsibility in AI development. The organization's ability to navigate controversies, adapt to challenges, and actively engage with the AI community underscores its role as a leader in the field. As OpenAI continues to contribute to the ongoing narrative of artificial intelligence, its journey serves as a beacon for responsible and transformative AI development that benefits humanity as a whole.

www.ingramcontent.com/pod-product-compliance
Lightning Source LLC
LaVergne TN
LVHW051658050326
832903LV00032B/3891

* 9 7 9 8 8 6 8 2 4 8 9 3 1 *